Self-Learning U.S. History & Geography with Creative Writing and Art

Workbook 1

by Randi L. Millward

ISBN-10: 1-943771-04-9
ISBN-13: 978-1-943771-04-2

Year 1

Preface

Welcome to the *Self-Learning U.S. History & Geography with Creative Writing and Art* curriculum.   This workbook is the first book in a 2-book 2-year self-learning curriculum, suitable for all school age children. Middle-schoolers and high-schoolers can work independently, while elementary students may work with assistance.

When the instructions say to choose a state to research, choose one that you haven't already researched in previous lessons. Choose a different state for each lesson. By choosing different states, all 50 states will be covered by the end of Year 2.

If the lines, pages, or blank areas provided for the writing or artwork is insufficient, feel free to use additional and/or larger sheets of paper.

To research, feel free to use books, the internet, or both. Interviewing someone who lives in the state you're researching would be educational as well.

Be creative with your writing and drawing. Make them projects of which you can be proud.

Most of all, enjoy the satisfaction and joy of taking charge of your own education with self-learning.

Happy learning!

Year 1

Year 1 - Week 1 - Day 1

Choose a state. Research that state, using books, the internet, or both. Make notes on the following lines. Include relevant information. Examples include, but are not limited to, the year it became a state, significant waterways, modes of transportation, its significance in any battles, discoveries or inventions by someone in that state, famous leaders that lived in or were born in that state, historical landmarks in that state, crops grown there, imports, exports, religious or cultural beliefs and practices, political views, laws, common occupations, cost of living, large cities, military bases, notable recipes, climate, geographical information such as elevation, population, or any information you find to be interesting. (You needn't include all of that information. Those are just examples and suggestions.)

_____

_____

_____

_____

_____

_____

_____

_____

_____

_____

_____

_____

_____

Year 1 - Week 1 - Day 2

Draw a map of the state. If you can't fit it onto this page, feel free to use a larger sheet of paper.

Year 1 - Week 1 - Day 3

In the box below, draw a historical landmark that is in the state you researched. On the lines below the box, write a little about the landmark you drew.

Year 1 - Week 1 - Day 4

On the following lines, write about what you liked and what you didn't like about the state you researched.

_____

_____

_____

_____

_____

_____

_____

_____

_____

_____

_____

_____

_____

_____

_____

Year 1 - Week 1 - Day 5

On the lines below, write about how the state you researched is different from and similar to the state in which you live. If the state you researched is the state in which you live, write about what you like about the community in which you live.

_____

_____

_____

_____

_____

_____

_____

_____

_____

_____

_____

_____

_____

_____

_____

_____

Year 1 - Week 2 - Day 1

Choose a state. Research that state, using books, the internet, or both. Make notes on the following lines. Include relevant information. Examples include, but are not limited to, the year it became a state, significant waterways, modes of transportation, its significance in any battles, discoveries or inventions by someone in that state, famous leaders that lived in or were born in that state, historical landmarks in that state, crops grown there, imports, exports, religious or cultural beliefs and practices, political views, laws, common occupations, cost of living, large cities, military bases, notable recipes, climate, geographical information such as elevation, population, or any information you find to be interesting. (You needn't include all of that information. Those are just examples and suggestions.)

_____

_____

_____

_____

_____

_____

_____

_____

_____

_____

_____

_____

_____

Year 1 - Week 2 - Day 2

Draw a map of the state. If you can't fit it onto this page, feel free to use a larger sheet of paper.

Year 1 - Week 2 - Day 3

In the box below, draw a historical landmark that is in the state you researched. On the lines below the box, write a little about the landmark you drew.

Year 1 - Week 2 - Day 4

On the following lines, write about what you liked and what you didn't like about the state you researched.

_____

_____

_____

_____

_____

_____

_____

_____

_____

_____

_____

_____

_____

_____

_____

_____

Year 1 - Week 2 - Day 5

On the lines below, write about how the state you researched is different from and similar to the state in which you live. If the state you researched is the state in which you live, write about what you like about the community in which you live.

_____

_____

_____

_____

_____

_____

_____

_____

_____

_____

_____

_____

_____

_____

_____

Year 1 - Week 3 - Day 1

Choose a state. Research that state, using books, the internet, or both. Make notes on the following lines. Include relevant information. Examples include, but are not limited to, the year it became a state, significant waterways, modes of transportation, its significance in any battles, discoveries or inventions by someone in that state, famous leaders that lived in or were born in that state, historical landmarks in that state, crops grown there, imports, exports, religious or cultural beliefs and practices, political views, laws, common occupations, cost of living, large cities, military bases, notable recipes, climate, geographical information such as elevation, population, or any information you find to be interesting. (You needn't include all of that information. Those are just examples and suggestions.)

_____

_____

_____

_____

_____

_____

_____

_____

_____

_____

_____

_____

_____

_____

Year 1 - Week 3 - Day 2

Draw a map of the state. If you can't fit it onto this page, feel free to use a larger sheet of paper.

Year 1 - Week 3 - Day 3

In the box below, draw a historical landmark that is in the state you researched. On the lines below the box, write a little about the landmark you drew.

_____

_____

_____

_____

_____

_____

Year 1 - Week 3 - Day 4

On the following lines, write about what you liked and what you didn't like about the state you researched.

_____

_____

_____

_____

_____

_____

_____

_____

_____

_____

_____

_____

_____

_____

_____

_____

Year 1 - Week 3 - Day 5

On the lines below, write about how the state you researched is different from and similar to the state in which you live. If the state you researched is the state in which you live, write about what you like about the community in which you live.

_____

_____

_____

_____

_____

_____

_____

_____

_____

_____

_____

_____

_____

_____

_____

Year 1 - Week 4 - Day 1

Choose a state. Research that state, using books, the internet, or both. Make notes on the following lines. Include relevant information. Examples include, but are not limited to, the year it became a state, significant waterways, modes of transportation, its significance in any battles, discoveries or inventions by someone in that state, famous leaders that lived in or were born in that state, historical landmarks in that state, crops grown there, imports, exports, religious or cultural beliefs and practices, political views, laws, common occupations, cost of living, large cities, military bases, notable recipes, climate, geographical information such as elevation, population, or any information you find to be interesting. (You needn't include all of that information. Those are just examples and suggestions.)

_____

_____

_____

_____

_____

_____

_____

_____

_____

_____

_____

_____

_____

_____

Year 1 - Week 4 - Day 2

Draw a map of the state. If you can't fit it onto this page, feel free to use a larger sheet of paper.

Year 1 - Week 4 - Day 3

In the box below, draw a historical landmark that is in the state you researched. On the lines below the box, write a little about the landmark you drew.

_____

_____

_____

_____

_____

_____

_____

Year 1 - Week 4 - Day 4

On the following lines, write about what you liked and what you didn't like about the state you researched.

_____

_____

_____

_____

_____

_____

_____

_____

_____

_____

_____

_____

_____

_____

_____

Year 1 - Week 4 - Day 5

On the lines below, write about how the state you researched is different from and similar to the state in which you live. If the state you researched is the state in which you live, write about what you like about the community in which you live.

_____

_____

_____

_____

_____

_____

_____

_____

_____

_____

_____

_____

_____

_____

_____

Year 1 - Week 5 - Day 1

Choose a state. Research that state, using books, the internet, or both. Make notes on the following lines. Include relevant information. Examples include, but are not limited to, the year it became a state, significant waterways, modes of transportation, its significance in any battles, discoveries or inventions by someone in that state, famous leaders that lived in or were born in that state, historical landmarks in that state, crops grown there, imports, exports, religious or cultural beliefs and practices, political views, laws, common occupations, cost of living, large cities, military bases, notable recipes, climate, geographical information such as elevation, population, or any information you find to be interesting. (You needn't include all of that information. Those are just examples and suggestions.)

_____

_____

_____

_____

_____

_____

_____

_____

_____

_____

_____

_____

_____

_____

Year 1 - Week 5 - Day 2

Draw a map of the state. If you can't fit it onto this page, feel free to use a larger sheet of paper.

Year 1 - Week 5 - Day 3

In the box below, draw a historical landmark that is in the state you researched. On the lines below the box, write a little about the landmark you drew.

_____

_____

_____

_____

_____

_____

Year 1 - Week 5 - Day 4

On the following lines, write about what you liked and what you didn't like about the state you researched.

_____

_____

_____

_____

_____

_____

_____

_____

_____

_____

_____

_____

_____

_____

_____

_____

Year 1 - Week 5 - Day 5

On the lines below, write about how the state you researched is different from and similar to the state in which you live. If the state you researched is the state in which you live, write about what you like about the community in which you live.

_____

_____

_____

_____

_____

_____

_____

_____

_____

_____

_____

_____

_____

_____

_____

_____

Year 1 - Week 6 - Day 1

Choose a state. Research that state, using books, the internet, or both. Make notes on the following lines. Include relevant information. Examples include, but are not limited to, the year it became a state, significant waterways, modes of transportation, its significance in any battles, discoveries or inventions by someone in that state, famous leaders that lived in or were born in that state, historical landmarks in that state, crops grown there, imports, exports, religious or cultural beliefs and practices, political views, laws, common occupations, cost of living, large cities, military bases, notable recipes, climate, geographical information such as elevation, population, or any information you find to be interesting. (You needn't include all of that information. Those are just examples and suggestions.)

_____

_____

_____

_____

_____

_____

_____

_____

_____

_____

_____

_____

_____

Year 1 - Week 6 - Day 2

Draw a map of the state. If you can't fit it onto this page, feel free to use a larger sheet of paper.

Year 1 - Week 6 - Day 3

In the box below, draw a historical landmark that is in the state you researched. On the lines below the box, write a little about the landmark you drew.

Year 1 - Week 6 - Day 4

On the following lines, write about what you liked and what you didn't like about the state you researched.

_____

_____

_____

_____

_____

_____

_____

_____

_____

_____

_____

_____

_____

_____

_____

_____

Year 1 - Week 6 - Day 5

On the lines below, write about how the state you researched is different from and similar to the state in which you live. If the state you researched is the state in which you live, write about what you like about the community in which you live.

_____

_____

_____

_____

_____

_____

_____

_____

_____

_____

_____

_____

_____

_____

_____

Year 1 - Week 7 - Day 1

Choose a state. Research that state, using books, the internet, or both. Make notes on the following lines. Include relevant information. Examples include, but are not limited to, the year it became a state, significant waterways, modes of transportation, its significance in any battles, discoveries or inventions by someone in that state, famous leaders that lived in or were born in that state, historical landmarks in that state, crops grown there, imports, exports, religious or cultural beliefs and practices, political views, laws, common occupations, cost of living, large cities, military bases, notable recipes, climate, geographical information such as elevation, population, or any information you find to be interesting. (You needn't include all of that information. Those are just examples and suggestions.)

_____

_____

_____

_____

_____

_____

_____

_____

_____

_____

_____

_____

_____

_____

Year 1 - Week 7 - Day 2

Draw a map of the state. If you can't fit it onto this page, feel free to use a larger sheet of paper.

Year 1 - Week 7 - Day 3

In the box below, draw a historical landmark that is in the state you researched. On the lines below the box, write a little about the landmark you drew.

_____

_____

_____

_____

_____

_____

Year 1 - Week 7 - Day 4

On the following lines, write about what you liked and what you didn't like about the state you researched.

_____

_____

_____

_____

_____

_____

_____

_____

_____

_____

_____

_____

_____

_____

_____

_____

_____

_____

Year 1 - Week 7 - Day 5

On the lines below, write about how the state you researched is different from and similar to the state in which you live. If the state you researched is the state in which you live, write about what you like about the community in which you live.

_____

_____

_____

_____

_____

_____

_____

_____

_____

_____

_____

_____

_____

_____

_____

_____

Year 1 - Week 8 - Day 1

Choose a state. Research that state, using books, the internet, or both. Make notes on the following lines. Include relevant information. Examples include, but are not limited to, the year it became a state, significant waterways, modes of transportation, its significance in any battles, discoveries or inventions by someone in that state, famous leaders that lived in or were born in that state, historical landmarks in that state, crops grown there, imports, exports, religious or cultural beliefs and practices, political views, laws, common occupations, cost of living, large cities, military bases, notable recipes, climate, geographical information such as elevation, population, or any information you find to be interesting. (You needn't include all of that information. Those are just examples and suggestions.)

_____

_____

_____

_____

_____

_____

_____

_____

_____

_____

_____

_____

_____

_____

_____

Year 1 - Week 8 - Day 2

Draw a map of the state. If you can't fit it onto this page, feel free to use a larger sheet of paper.

Year 1 - Week 8 - Day 3

In the box below, draw a historical landmark that is in the state you researched. On the lines below the box, write a little about the landmark you drew.

_____

_____

_____

_____

_____

_____

Year 1 - Week 8 - Day 4

On the following lines, write about what you liked and what you didn't like about the state you researched.

_____

_____

_____

_____

_____

_____

_____

_____

_____

_____

_____

_____

_____

_____

_____

_____

Year 1 - Week 8 - Day 5

On the lines below, write about how the state you researched is different from and similar to the state in which you live. If the state you researched is the state in which you live, write about what you like about the community in which you live.

_____

_____

_____

_____

_____

_____

_____

_____

_____

_____

_____

_____

_____

_____

_____

_____

Year 1 - Week 8 - Day 1

Choose a state. Research that state, using books, the internet, or both. Make notes on the following lines. Include relevant information. Examples include, but are not limited to, the year it became a state, significant waterways, modes of transportation, its significance in any battles, discoveries or inventions by someone in that state, famous leaders that lived in or were born in that state, historical landmarks in that state, crops grown there, imports, exports, religious or cultural beliefs and practices, political views, laws, common occupations, cost of living, large cities, military bases, notable recipes, climate, geographical information such as elevation, population, or any information you find to be interesting. (You needn't include all of that information. Those are just examples and suggestions.)

_____

_____

_____

_____

_____

_____

_____

_____

_____

_____

_____

_____

_____

_____

<u>Year 1 - Week 8 - Day 2</u>

Draw a map of the state. If you can't fit it onto this page, feel free to use a larger sheet of paper.

Year 1 - Week 8 - Day 3

In the box below, draw a historical landmark that is in the state you researched. On the lines below the box, write a little about the landmark you drew.

Year 1 - Week 8 - Day 4

On the following lines, write about what you liked and what you didn't like about the state you researched.

_____

_____

_____

_____

_____

_____

_____

_____

_____

_____

_____

_____

_____

_____

_____

_____

Year 1 - Week 8 - Day 5

On the lines below, write about how the state you researched is different from and similar to the state in which you live. If the state you researched is the state in which you live, write about what you like about the community in which you live.

_____

_____

_____

_____

_____

_____

_____

_____

_____

_____

_____

_____

_____

_____

_____

Year 1 - Week 9 - Day 1

Choose a state. Research that state, using books, the internet, or both. Make notes on the following lines. Include relevant information. Examples include, but are not limited to, the year it became a state, significant waterways, modes of transportation, its significance in any battles, discoveries or inventions by someone in that state, famous leaders that lived in or were born in that state, historical landmarks in that state, crops grown there, imports, exports, religious or cultural beliefs and practices, political views, laws, common occupations, cost of living, large cities, military bases, notable recipes, climate, geographical information such as elevation, population, or any information you find to be interesting. (You needn't include all of that information. Those are just examples and suggestions.)

_____

_____

_____

_____

_____

_____

_____

_____

_____

_____

_____

_____

_____

_____

Year 1 - Week 9 - Day 2

Draw a map of the state. If you can't fit it onto this page, feel free to use a larger sheet of paper.

Year 1 - Week 9 - Day 3

In the box below, draw a historical landmark that is in the state you researched. On the lines below the box, write a little about the landmark you drew.

_____

_____

_____

_____

_____

_____

Year 1 - Week 9 - Day 4

On the following lines, write about what you liked and what you didn't like about the state you researched.

_____

_____

_____

_____

_____

_____

_____

_____

_____

_____

_____

_____

_____

_____

_____

_____

_____

_____

Year 1 - Week 9 - Day 5

On the lines below, write about how the state you researched is different from and similar to the state in which you live. If the state you researched is the state in which you live, write about what you like about the community in which you live.

_____

_____

_____

_____

_____

_____

_____

_____

_____

_____

_____

_____

_____

_____

_____

_____

_____

Year 1 - Week 10 - Day 1

Choose a state. Research that state, using books, the internet, or both. Make notes on the following lines. Include relevant information. Examples include, but are not limited to, the year it became a state, significant waterways, modes of transportation, its significance in any battles, discoveries or inventions by someone in that state, famous leaders that lived in or were born in that state, historical landmarks in that state, crops grown there, imports, exports, religious or cultural beliefs and practices, political views, laws, common occupations, cost of living, large cities, military bases, notable recipes, climate, geographical information such as elevation, population, or any information you find to be interesting. (You needn't include all of that information. Those are just examples and suggestions.)

_____

_____

_____

_____

_____

_____

_____

_____

_____

_____

_____

_____

_____

Year 1 - Week 10 - Day 2

Draw a map of the state. If you can't fit it onto this page, feel free to use a larger sheet of paper.

Year 1 - Week 10 - Day 3

In the box below, draw a historical landmark that is in the state you researched. On the lines below the box, write a little about the landmark you drew.

_____

_____

_____

_____

_____

_____

Year 1 - Week 10 - Day 4

On the following lines, write about what you liked and what you didn't like about the state you researched.

_____

_____

_____

_____

_____

_____

_____

_____

_____

_____

_____

_____

_____

_____

_____

_____

_____

Year 1 - Week 10 - Day 5

On the lines below, write about how the state you researched is different from and similar to the state in which you live. If the state you researched is the state in which you live, write about what you like about the community in which you live.

_____

_____

_____

_____

_____

_____

_____

_____

_____

_____

_____

_____

_____

_____

_____

_____

<u>Year 1 - Week 11 - Day 1</u>

Choose a state. Research that state, using books, the internet, or both. Make notes on the following lines. Include relevant information. Examples include, but are not limited to, the year it became a state, significant waterways, modes of transportation, its significance in any battles, discoveries or inventions by someone in that state, famous leaders that lived in or were born in that state, historical landmarks in that state, crops grown there, imports, exports, religious or cultural beliefs and practices, political views, laws, common occupations, cost of living, large cities, military bases, notable recipes, climate, geographical information such as elevation, population, or any information you find to be interesting. (You needn't include all of that information. Those are just examples and suggestions.)

_____

_____

_____

_____

_____

_____

_____

_____

_____

_____

_____

_____

_____

_____

Year 1 - Week 11 - Day 2

Draw a map of the state. If you can't fit it onto this page, feel free to use a larger sheet of paper.

Year 1 - Week 11 - Day 3

In the box below, draw a historical landmark that is in the state you researched. On the lines below the box, write a little about the landmark you drew.

_____

_____

_____

_____

_____

_____

Year 1 - Week 11 - Day 4

On the following lines, write about what you liked and what you didn't like about the state you researched.

_____

_____

_____

_____

_____

_____

_____

_____

_____

_____

_____

_____

_____

_____

_____

_____

_____

Year 1 - Week 11 - Day 5

On the lines below, write about how the state you researched is different from and similar to the state in which you live. If the state you researched is the state in which you live, write about what you like about the community in which you live.

_____

_____

_____

_____

_____

_____

_____

_____

_____

_____

_____

_____

_____

_____

_____

Year 1 - Week 12 - Day 1

Choose a state. Research that state, using books, the internet, or both. Make notes on the following lines. Include relevant information. Examples include, but are not limited to, the year it became a state, significant waterways, modes of transportation, its significance in any battles, discoveries or inventions by someone in that state, famous leaders that lived in or were born in that state, historical landmarks in that state, crops grown there, imports, exports, religious or cultural beliefs and practices, political views, laws, common occupations, cost of living, large cities, military bases, notable recipes, climate, geographical information such as elevation, population, or any information you find to be interesting. (You needn't include all of that information. Those are just examples and suggestions.)

_____

_____

_____

_____

_____

_____

_____

_____

_____

_____

_____

_____

_____

Year 1 - Week 12 - Day 2

Draw a map of the state. If you can't fit it onto this page, feel free to use a larger sheet of paper.

Year 1 - Week 12 - Day 3

In the box below, draw a historical landmark that is in the state you researched. On the lines below the box, write a little about the landmark you drew.

_____

_____

_____

_____

_____

_____

Year 1 - Week 12 - Day 4

On the following lines, write about what you liked and what you didn't like about the state you researched.

_____

_____

_____

_____

_____

_____

_____

_____

_____

_____

_____

_____

_____

_____

_____

_____

_____

Year 1 - Week 12 - Day 5

On the lines below, write about how the state you researched is different from and similar to the state in which you live. If the state you researched is the state in which you live, write about what you like about the community in which you live.

_____

_____

_____

_____

_____

_____

_____

_____

_____

_____

_____

_____

_____

_____

_____

_____

_____

Year 1 - Week 13 - Day 1

Choose a state. Research that state, using books, the internet, or both. Make notes on the following lines. Include relevant information. Examples include, but are not limited to, the year it became a state, significant waterways, modes of transportation, its significance in any battles, discoveries or inventions by someone in that state, famous leaders that lived in or were born in that state, historical landmarks in that state, crops grown there, imports, exports, religious or cultural beliefs and practices, political views, laws, common occupations, cost of living, large cities, military bases, notable recipes, climate, geographical information such as elevation, population, or any information you find to be interesting. (You needn't include all of that information. Those are just examples and suggestions.)

_____

_____

_____

_____

_____

_____

_____

_____

_____

_____

_____

_____

_____

Year 1 - Week 13 - Day 2

Draw a map of the state. If you can't fit it onto this page, feel free to use a larger sheet of paper.

Year 1 - Week 13 - Day 3

In the box below, draw a historical landmark that is in the state you researched. On the lines below the box, write a little about the landmark you drew.

_____

_____

_____

_____

_____

_____

Year 1 - Week 13 - Day 4

On the following lines, write about what you liked and what you didn't like about the state you researched.

_____

_____

_____

_____

_____

_____

_____

_____

_____

_____

_____

_____

_____

_____

_____

Year 1 - Week 13 - Day 5

On the lines below, write about how the state you researched is different from and similar to the state in which you live. If the state you researched is the state in which you live, write about what you like about the community in which you live.

_____

_____

_____

_____

_____

_____

_____

_____

_____

_____

_____

_____

_____

_____

_____

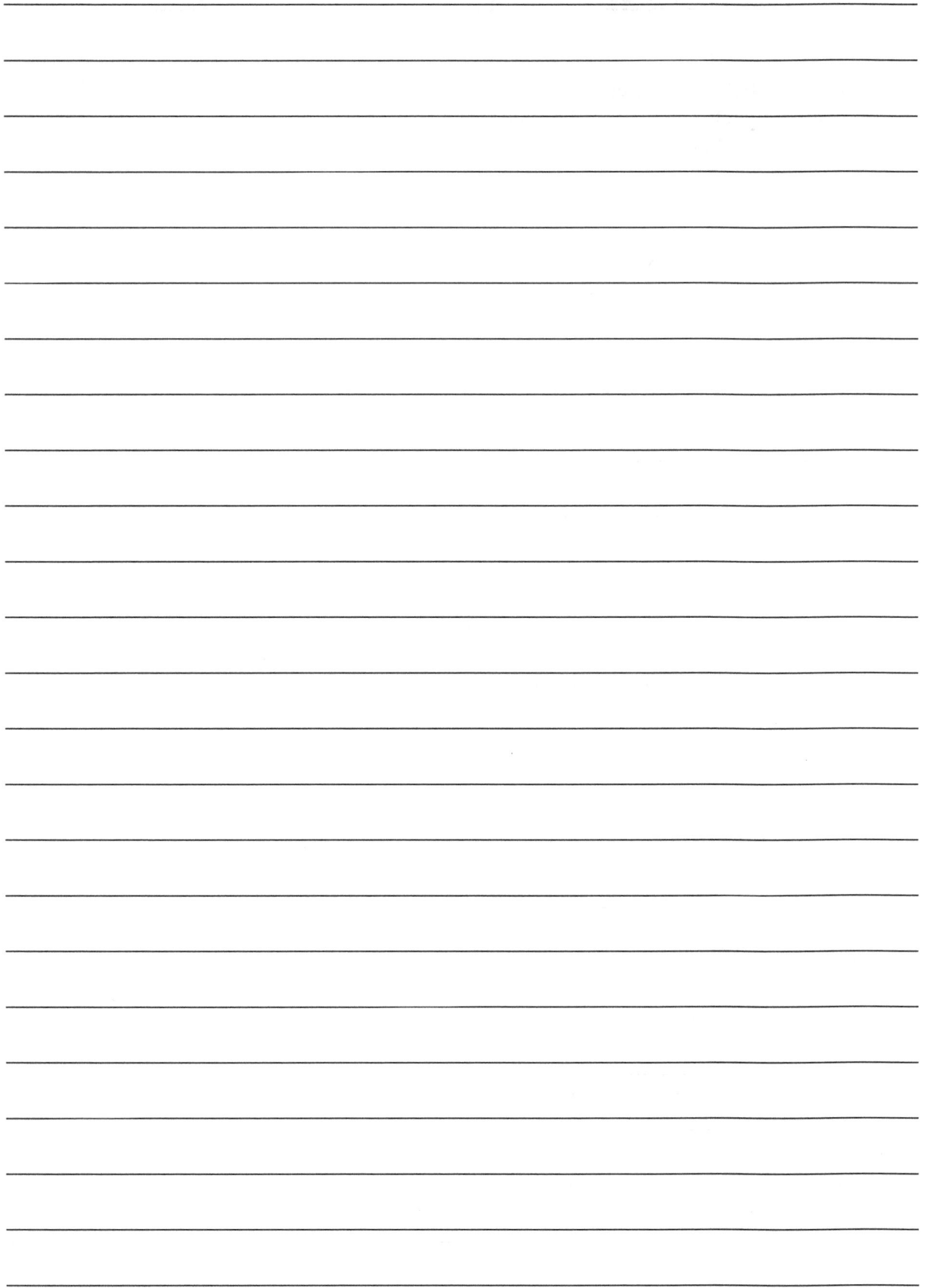

Year 1 - Week 14 - Day 1

Choose a state. Research that state, using books, the internet, or both. Make notes on the following lines. Include relevant information. Examples include, but are not limited to, the year it became a state, significant waterways, modes of transportation, its significance in any battles, discoveries or inventions by someone in that state, famous leaders that lived in or were born in that state, historical landmarks in that state, crops grown there, imports, exports, religious or cultural beliefs and practices, political views, laws, common occupations, cost of living, large cities, military bases, notable recipes, climate, geographical information such as elevation, population, or any information you find to be interesting. (You needn't include all of that information. Those are just examples and suggestions.)

_____

_____

_____

_____

_____

_____

_____

_____

_____

_____

_____

_____

_____

Year 1 - Week 14 - Day 2

Draw a map of the state. If you can't fit it onto this page, feel free to use a larger sheet of paper.

Year 1 - Week 14 - Day 3

In the box below, draw a historical landmark that is in the state you researched. On the lines below the box, write a little about the landmark you drew.

Year 1 - Week 14 - Day 4

On the following lines, write about what you liked and what you didn't like about the state you researched.

_____

_____

_____

_____

_____

_____

_____

_____

_____

_____

_____

_____

_____

_____

_____

_____

Year 1 - Week 14 - Day 5

On the lines below, write about how the state you researched is different from and similar to the state in which you live. If the state you researched is the state in which you live, write about what you like about the community in which you live.

_____

_____

_____

_____

_____

_____

_____

_____

_____

_____

_____

_____

_____

_____

_____

_____

_____

Year 1 - Week 15 - Day 1

Choose a state. Research that state, using books, the internet, or both. Make notes on the following lines. Include relevant information. Examples include, but are not limited to, the year it became a state, significant waterways, modes of transportation, its significance in any battles, discoveries or inventions by someone in that state, famous leaders that lived in or were born in that state, historical landmarks in that state, crops grown there, imports, exports, religious or cultural beliefs and practices, political views, laws, common occupations, cost of living, large cities, military bases, notable recipes, climate, geographical information such as elevation, population, or any information you find to be interesting. (You needn't include all of that information. Those are just examples and suggestions.)

_____

_____

_____

_____

_____

_____

_____

_____

_____

_____

_____

_____

_____

_____

Year 1 - Week 15 - Day 2

Draw a map of the state. If you can't fit it onto this page, feel free to use a larger sheet of paper.

Year 1 - Week 15 - Day 3

In the box below, draw a historical landmark that is in the state you researched. On the lines below the box, write a little about the landmark you drew.

[Drawing box — empty]

_____

_____

_____

_____

_____

_____

Year 1 - Week 15 - Day 4

On the following lines, write about what you liked and what you didn't like about the state you researched.

_____

_____

_____

_____

_____

_____

_____

_____

_____

_____

_____

_____

_____

_____

_____

_____

_____

_____

Year 1 - Week 15 - Day 5

On the lines below, write about how the state you researched is different from and similar to the state in which you live. If the state you researched is the state in which you live, write about what you like about the community in which you live.

_____

_____

_____

_____

_____

_____

_____

_____

_____

_____

_____

_____

_____

_____

_____

_____

_____

Year 1 - Week 16 - Day 1

Choose a state. Research that state, using books, the internet, or both. Make notes on the following lines. Include relevant information. Examples include, but are not limited to, the year it became a state, significant waterways, modes of transportation, its significance in any battles, discoveries or inventions by someone in that state, famous leaders that lived in or were born in that state, historical landmarks in that state, crops grown there, imports, exports, religious or cultural beliefs and practices, political views, laws, common occupations, cost of living, large cities, military bases, notable recipes, climate, geographical information such as elevation, population, or any information you find to be interesting. (You needn't include all of that information. Those are just examples and suggestions.)

_____

_____

_____

_____

_____

_____

_____

_____

_____

_____

_____

_____

_____

_____

Year 1 - Week 16 - Day 2

Draw a map of the state. If you can't fit it onto this page, feel free to use a larger sheet of paper.

Year 1 - Week 16 - Day 3

In the box below, draw a historical landmark that is in the state you researched. On the lines below the box, write a little about the landmark you drew.

_____

_____

_____

_____

_____

_____

Year 1 - Week 16 - Day 4

On the following lines, write about what you liked and what you didn't like about the state you researched.

_____

_____

_____

_____

_____

_____

_____

_____

_____

_____

_____

_____

_____

_____

_____

_____

_____

Year 1 - Week 16 - Day 5

On the lines below, write about how the state you researched is different from and similar to the state in which you live. If the state you researched is the state in which you live, write about what you like about the community in which you live.

_____

_____

_____

_____

_____

_____

_____

_____

_____

_____

_____

_____

_____

_____

_____

_____

Year 1 - Week 17 - Day 1

Choose a state. Research that state, using books, the internet, or both. Make notes on the following lines. Include relevant information. Examples include, but are not limited to, the year it became a state, significant waterways, modes of transportation, its significance in any battles, discoveries or inventions by someone in that state, famous leaders that lived in or were born in that state, historical landmarks in that state, crops grown there, imports, exports, religious or cultural beliefs and practices, political views, laws, common occupations, cost of living, large cities, military bases, notable recipes, climate, geographical information such as elevation, population, or any information you find to be interesting. (You needn't include all of that information. Those are just examples and suggestions.)

_____

_____

_____

_____

_____

_____

_____

_____

_____

_____

_____

_____

_____

_____

_____

Year 1 - Week 17 - Day 2

Draw a map of the state. If you can't fit it onto this page, feel free to use a larger sheet of paper.

Year 1 - Week 17 - Day 3

In the box below, draw a historical landmark that is in the state you researched. On the lines below the box, write a little about the landmark you drew.

_____

_____

_____

_____

_____

_____

Year 1 - Week 17 - Day 4

On the following lines, write about what you liked and what you didn't like about the state you researched.

_____

_____

_____

_____

_____

_____

_____

_____

_____

_____

_____

_____

_____

_____

_____

_____

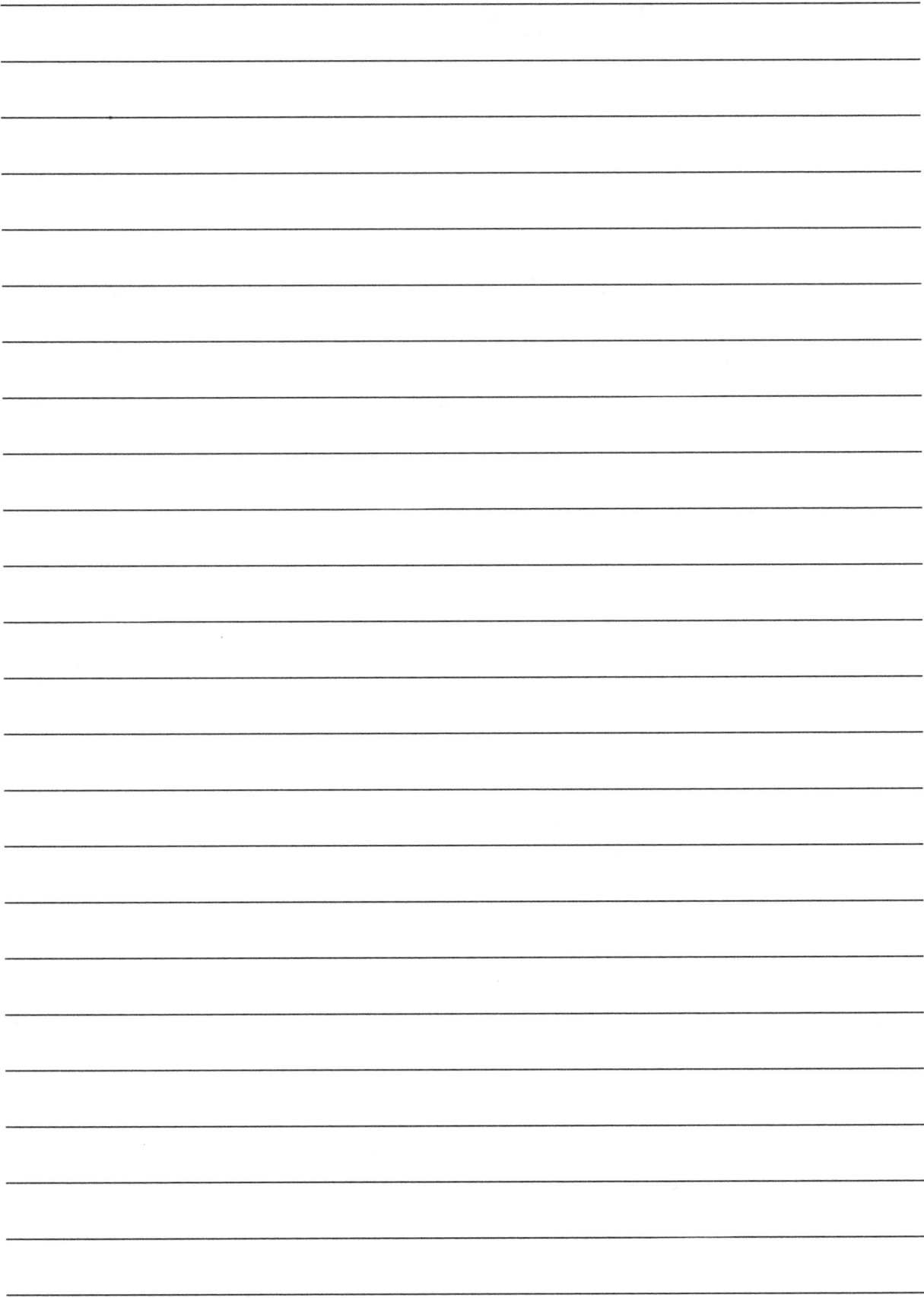

Year 1 - Week 17 - Day 5

On the lines below, write about how the state you researched is different from and similar to the state in which you live. If the state you researched is the state in which you live, write about what you like about the community in which you live.

_____

_____

_____

_____

_____

_____

_____

_____

_____

_____

_____

_____

_____

_____

_____

Year 1 - Week 18 - Day 1

Choose a state. Research that state, using books, the internet, or both. Make notes on the following lines. Include relevant information. Examples include, but are not limited to, the year it became a state, significant waterways, modes of transportation, its significance in any battles, discoveries or inventions by someone in that state, famous leaders that lived in or were born in that state, historical landmarks in that state, crops grown there, imports, exports, religious or cultural beliefs and practices, political views, laws, common occupations, cost of living, large cities, military bases, notable recipes, climate, geographical information such as elevation, population, or any information you find to be interesting. (You needn't include all of that information. Those are just examples and suggestions.)

_____

_____

_____

_____

_____

_____

_____

_____

_____

_____

_____

_____

_____

Year 1 - Week 18 - Day 2

Draw a map of the state. If you can't fit it onto this page, feel free to use a larger sheet of paper.

Year 1 - Week 18 - Day 3

In the box below, draw a historical landmark that is in the state you researched. On the lines below the box, write a little about the landmark you drew.

_____

_____

_____

_____

_____

_____

Year 1 - Week 18 - Day 4

On the following lines, write about what you liked and what you didn't like about the state you researched.

_____

_____

_____

_____

_____

_____

_____

_____

_____

_____

_____

_____

_____

_____

_____

_____

Year 1 - Week 18 - Day 5

On the lines below, write about how the state you researched is different from and similar to the state in which you live. If the state you researched is the state in which you live, write about what you like about the community in which you live.

_____

_____

_____

_____

_____

_____

_____

_____

_____

_____

_____

_____

_____

_____

_____

_____

Year 1 - Week 19 - Day 1

Choose a state. Research that state, using books, the internet, or both. Make notes on the following lines. Include relevant information. Examples include, but are not limited to, the year it became a state, significant waterways, modes of transportation, its significance in any battles, discoveries or inventions by someone in that state, famous leaders that lived in or were born in that state, historical landmarks in that state, crops grown there, imports, exports, religious or cultural beliefs and practices, political views, laws, common occupations, cost of living, large cities, military bases, notable recipes, climate, geographical information such as elevation, population, or any information you find to be interesting. (You needn't include all of that information. Those are just examples and suggestions.)

_____

_____

_____

_____

_____

_____

_____

_____

_____

_____

_____

_____

_____

_____

Year 1 - Week 19 - Day 2

Draw a map of the state. If you can't fit it onto this page, feel free to use a larger sheet of paper.

Year 1 - Week 19 - Day 3

In the box below, draw a historical landmark that is in the state you researched. On the lines below the box, write a little about the landmark you drew.

_____

_____

_____

_____

_____

_____

Year 1 - Week 19 - Day 4

On the following lines, write about what you liked and what you didn't like about the state you researched.

_____

_____

_____

_____

_____

_____

_____

_____

_____

_____

_____

_____

_____

_____

_____

_____

Year 1 - Week 19 - Day 5

On the lines below, write about how the state you researched is different from and similar to the state in which you live. If the state you researched is the state in which you live, write about what you like about the community in which you live.

_____

_____

_____

_____

_____

_____

_____

_____

_____

_____

_____

_____

_____

_____

_____

Year 1 - Week 20 - Day 1

Choose a state. Research that state, using books, the internet, or both. Make notes on the following lines. Include relevant information. Examples include, but are not limited to, the year it became a state, significant waterways, modes of transportation, its significance in any battles, discoveries or inventions by someone in that state, famous leaders that lived in or were born in that state, historical landmarks in that state, crops grown there, imports, exports, religious or cultural beliefs and practices, political views, laws, common occupations, cost of living, large cities, military bases, notable recipes, climate, geographical information such as elevation, population, or any information you find to be interesting. (You needn't include all of that information. Those are just examples and suggestions.)

_____

_____

_____

_____

_____

_____

_____

_____

_____

_____

_____

_____

_____

_____

Year 1 - Week 20 - Day 2

Draw a map of the state. If you can't fit it onto this page, feel free to use a larger sheet of paper.

Year 1 - Week 20 - Day 3

In the box below, draw a historical landmark that is in the state you researched. On the lines below the box, write a little about the landmark you drew.

_____

_____

_____

_____

_____

_____

Year 1 - Week 20 - Day 4

On the following lines, write about what you liked and what you didn't like about the state you researched.

_____

_____

_____

_____

_____

_____

_____

_____

_____

_____

_____

_____

_____

_____

_____

Year 1 - Week 20 - Day 5

On the lines below, write about how the state you researched is different from and similar to the state in which you live. If the state you researched is the state in which you live, write about what you like about the community in which you live.

_____

_____

_____

_____

_____

_____

_____

_____

_____

_____

_____

_____

_____

_____

_____

Year 1 - Week 21 - Day 1

Choose a state. Research that state, using books, the internet, or both. Make notes on the following lines. Include relevant information. Examples include, but are not limited to, the year it became a state, significant waterways, modes of transportation, its significance in any battles, discoveries or inventions by someone in that state, famous leaders that lived in or were born in that state, historical landmarks in that state, crops grown there, imports, exports, religious or cultural beliefs and practices, political views, laws, common occupations, cost of living, large cities, military bases, notable recipes, climate, geographical information such as elevation, population, or any information you find to be interesting. (You needn't include all of that information. Those are just examples and suggestions.)

_____

_____

_____

_____

_____

_____

_____

_____

_____

_____

_____

_____

_____

Year 1 - Week 21 - Day 2

Draw a map of the state. If you can't fit it onto this page, feel free to use a larger sheet of paper.

Year 1 - Week 21 - Day 3

In the box below, draw a historical landmark that is in the state you researched. On the lines below the box, write a little about the landmark you drew.

_____

_____

_____

_____

_____

_____

Year 1 - Week 21 - Day 4

On the following lines, write about what you liked and what you didn't like about the state you researched.

_____

_____

_____

_____

_____

_____

_____

_____

_____

_____

_____

_____

_____

_____

_____

_____

Year 1 - Week 21 - Day 5

On the lines below, write about how the state you researched is different from and similar to the state in which you live. If the state you researched is the state in which you live, write about what you like about the community in which you live.

_____

_____

_____

_____

_____

_____

_____

_____

_____

_____

_____

_____

_____

_____

_____

Year 1 - Week 22 - Day 1

Choose a state. Research that state, using books, the internet, or both. Make notes on the following lines. Include relevant information. Examples include, but are not limited to, the year it became a state, significant waterways, modes of transportation, its significance in any battles, discoveries or inventions by someone in that state, famous leaders that lived in or were born in that state, historical landmarks in that state, crops grown there, imports, exports, religious or cultural beliefs and practices, political views, laws, common occupations, cost of living, large cities, military bases, notable recipes, climate, geographical information such as elevation, population, or any information you find to be interesting. (You needn't include all of that information. Those are just examples and suggestions.)

_____

_____

_____

_____

_____

_____

_____

_____

_____

_____

_____

_____

_____

_____

Year 1 - Week 22 - Day 2

Draw a map of the state. If you can't fit it onto this page, feel free to use a larger sheet of paper.

Year 1 - Week 22 - Day 3

In the box below, draw a historical landmark that is in the state you researched. On the lines below the box, write a little about the landmark you drew.

_____

_____

_____

_____

_____

_____

_____

Year 1 - Week 22 - Day 4

On the following lines, write about what you liked and what you didn't like about the state you researched.

_____

_____

_____

_____

_____

_____

_____

_____

_____

_____

_____

_____

_____

_____

_____

_____

_____

Year 1 - Week 22 - Day 5

On the lines below, write about how the state you researched is different from and similar to the state in which you live. If the state you researched is the state in which you live, write about what you like about the community in which you live.

_____

_____

_____

_____

_____

_____

_____

_____

_____

_____

_____

_____

_____

_____

_____

Year 1 - Week 23 - Day 1

Choose a state. Research that state, using books, the internet, or both. Make notes on the following lines. Include relevant information. Examples include, but are not limited to, the year it became a state, significant waterways, modes of transportation, its significance in any battles, discoveries or inventions by someone in that state, famous leaders that lived in or were born in that state, historical landmarks in that state, crops grown there, imports, exports, religious or cultural beliefs and practices, political views, laws, common occupations, cost of living, large cities, military bases, notable recipes, climate, geographical information such as elevation, population, or any information you find to be interesting. (You needn't include all of that information. Those are just examples and suggestions.)

_____

_____

_____

_____

_____

_____

_____

_____

_____

_____

_____

_____

_____

Year 1 - Week 23 - Day 2

Draw a map of the state. If you can't fit it onto this page, feel free to use a larger sheet of paper.

Year 1 - Week 23 - Day 3

In the box below, draw a historical landmark that is in the state you researched. On the lines below the box, write a little about the landmark you drew.

_____

_____

_____

_____

_____

_____

Year 1 - Week 23 - Day 4

On the following lines, write about what you liked and what you didn't like about the state you researched.

_____

_____

_____

_____

_____

_____

_____

_____

_____

_____

_____

_____

_____

_____

_____

_____

Year 1 - Week 23 - Day 5

On the lines below, write about how the state you researched is different from and similar to the state in which you live. If the state you researched is the state in which you live, write about what you like about the community in which you live.

_____

_____

_____

_____

_____

_____

_____

_____

_____

_____

_____

_____

_____

_____

_____

_____

Year 1 - Week 24 - Day 1

Choose a state. Research that state, using books, the internet, or both. Make notes on the following lines. Include relevant information. Examples include, but are not limited to, the year it became a state, significant waterways, modes of transportation, its significance in any battles, discoveries or inventions by someone in that state, famous leaders that lived in or were born in that state, historical landmarks in that state, crops grown there, imports, exports, religious or cultural beliefs and practices, political views, laws, common occupations, cost of living, large cities, military bases, notable recipes, climate, geographical information such as elevation, population, or any information you find to be interesting. (You needn't include all of that information. Those are just examples and suggestions.)

_____

_____

_____

_____

_____

_____

_____

_____

_____

_____

_____

_____

_____

_____

Year 1 - Week 24 - Day 2

Draw a map of the state. If you can't fit it onto this page, feel free to use a larger sheet of paper.

Year 1 - Week 24 - Day 3

In the box below, draw a historical landmark that is in the state you researched. On the lines below the box, write a little about the landmark you drew.

_____

_____

_____

_____

_____

_____

Year 1 - Week 24 - Day 4

On the following lines, write about what you liked and what you didn't like about the state you researched.

_____

_____

_____

_____

_____

_____

_____

_____

_____

_____

_____

_____

_____

_____

_____

_____

Year 1 - Week 24 - Day 5

On the lines below, write about how the state you researched is different from and similar to the state in which you live. If the state you researched is the state in which you live, write about what you like about the community in which you live.

_____

_____

_____

_____

_____

_____

_____

_____

_____

_____

_____

_____

_____

_____

_____

_____

_____

Year 1 - Week 25 - Day 1

Choose a state. Research that state, using books, the internet, or both. Make notes on the following lines. Include relevant information. Examples include, but are not limited to, the year it became a state, significant waterways, modes of transportation, its significance in any battles, discoveries or inventions by someone in that state, famous leaders that lived in or were born in that state, historical landmarks in that state, crops grown there, imports, exports, religious or cultural beliefs and practices, political views, laws, common occupations, cost of living, large cities, military bases, notable recipes, climate, geographical information such as elevation, population, or any information you find to be interesting. (You needn't include all of that information. Those are just examples and suggestions.)

_____

_____

_____

_____

_____

_____

_____

_____

_____

_____

_____

_____

_____

_____

_____

Year 1 - Week 25 - Day 2

Draw a map of the state. If you can't fit it onto this page, feel free to use a larger sheet of paper.

Year 1 - Week 25 - Day 3

In the box below, draw a historical landmark that is in the state you researched. On the lines below the box, write a little about the landmark you drew.

_____

_____

_____

_____

_____

_____

Year 1 - Week 25 - Day 4

On the following lines, write about what you liked and what you didn't like about the state you researched.

_____

_____

_____

_____

_____

_____

_____

_____

_____

_____

_____

_____

_____

_____

_____

_____

_____

Year 1 - Week 25 - Day 5

On the lines below, write about how the state you researched is different from and similar to the state in which you live. If the state you researched is the state in which you live, write about what you like about the community in which you live.

_____

_____

_____

_____

_____

_____

_____

_____

_____

_____

_____

_____

_____

_____

Year 1 - Week 26 - Day 1

Review your research up to this point. Decide on the state you find to be most interesting to you. Write the name of the state on the line below.

_____

You will be writing about this state for the rest of the week.

Year 1 - Week 26 - Day 2

On the following lines, write what you find most interesting about the state that you chose yesterday.

_____

_____

_____

_____

_____

_____

_____

_____

_____

_____

_____

_____

_____

_____

_____

Year 1 - Week 26 - Day 3

On the following lines, compare and contrast your state with the state you wrote about yesterday.

_____

_____

_____

_____

_____

_____

_____

_____

_____

_____

_____

_____

_____

_____

_____

_____

Year 1 - Week 26 - Day 4

Pretend you live in the state that you chose to write about on Day 1 of this week. On the following lines, write about what an ordinary day would be like for you.

_____

_____

_____

_____

_____

_____

_____

_____

_____

_____

_____

_____

_____

_____

_____

_____

Year 1 - Week 26 - Day 5

Again, use the state that you chose to write about on Day 1 of this week. On the following lines, write about how your life would be different from how it is now if you lived in that state.

_____

_____

_____

_____

_____

_____

_____

_____

_____

_____

_____

_____

_____

_____

_____

_____

Year 1 - Week 27 - Days 1-5

Draw a map of the United States. If there is not enough room on this page, feel free to use a larger sheet of paper. This is a large project, so you will be working on it all week.

Year 1 - Week 28 - Day 1

Review your research up to this point. Decide on the landmark you find to be most interesting to you. Write the name and location of the landmark on the line below.

_____

You will be writing about this landmark for the rest of the week.

Year 1 - Week 28 - Day 2

On the following lines, write what you find most interesting about the landmark that you chose yesterday.

_____

_____

_____

_____

_____

_____

_____

_____

_____

_____

_____

_____

_____

_____

_____

_____

Year 1 - Week 28 - Day 3

Pretend you are going to visit the landmark that you chose to write about on Day 1 of this week. On the following lines, write what you would pack to bring on your trip and why.

_____

_____

_____

_____

_____

_____

_____

_____

_____

_____

_____

_____

_____

_____

_____

Year 1 - Week 28 - Day 4

Pretend you are going to visit the landmark that you chose to write about on Day 1 of this week. On the following lines, write how you would get to that landmark.

_____

_____

_____

_____

_____

_____

_____

_____

_____

_____

_____

_____

_____

_____

_____

_____

Year 1 - Week 28 - Day 5

Draw a picture of the landmark that you chose on Day 1 of this week.

Year 1 - Week 29 - Day 1

Review your research up to this point. Choose two different states that you've researched to write about this week.   Write the names of the states on the line below.

_____

You will be writing about these states for the rest of the week.

Year 1 - Week 29 - Day 2

On the following lines, write what you find most interesting about the states that you chose yesterday.

_____

_____

_____

_____

_____

_____

_____

_____

_____

_____

_____

_____

_____

_____

_____

_____

_____

Year 1 - Week 29 - Day 3

On the following lines, list similarities between the two states that you chose on Day 1 of this week.

_____

_____

_____

_____

_____

_____

_____

_____

_____

_____

_____

_____

_____

_____

_____

_____

Year 1 - Week 29 - Day 4

On the following lines, list differences between the two states that you chose on Day 1 of this week.

_____

_____

_____

_____

_____

_____

_____

_____

_____

_____

_____

_____

_____

_____

_____

_____

_____

Year 1 - Week 29 - Day 5

Draw a map showing how to get from one of the states you chose on Day 1 of this week to the other state you chose. If there isn't enough room on this page, feel free to use a larger paper.

Year 1 - Week 30 - Day 1

Review your research up to this point. Choose one northern state and one southern state that you've researched to write about this week. Write the names of the states on the line below.

_____

You will be writing about these states for the rest of the week.

Year 1 - Week 30 - Day 2

On the following lines, write what you find most interesting about the states that you chose yesterday.

_____

_____

_____

_____

_____

_____

_____

_____

_____

_____

_____

_____

_____

_____

_____

_____

_____

Year 1 - Week 30 - Day 3

On the following lines, list similarities between the two states that you chose on Day 1 of this week.

_____

_____

_____

_____

_____

_____

_____

_____

_____

_____

_____

_____

_____

_____

_____

Year 1 - Week 30 - Day 4

On the following lines, list differences between the two states that you chose on Day 1 of this week.

_____

_____

_____

_____

_____

_____

_____

_____

_____

_____

_____

_____

_____

_____

_____

_____

Year 1 - Week 30 - Day 5

Draw a map showing how to get from one of the states you chose on Day 1 of this week to the other state you chose. If there isn't enough room on this page, feel free to use a larger paper.

Year 1 - Week 31 - Day 1

Review your research up to this point. Choose one western state and one eastern state that you've researched to write about this week. Write the names of the states on the line below.

_____

You will be writing about these states for the rest of the week.

Year 1 - Week 31 - Day 2

On the following lines, write what you find most interesting about the states that you chose yesterday.

_____

_____

_____

_____

_____

_____

_____

_____

_____

_____

_____

_____

_____

_____

_____

_____

Year 1 - Week 31 - Day 3

On the following lines, list similarities between the two states that you chose on Day 1 of this week.

_____

_____

_____

_____

_____

_____

_____

_____

_____

_____

_____

_____

_____

_____

_____

_____

Year 1 - Week 31 - Day 4

On the following lines, list differences between the two states that you chose on Day 1 of this week.

_____

_____

_____

_____

_____

_____

_____

_____

_____

_____

_____

_____

_____

_____

_____

_____

Year 1 - Week 31 - Day 5

Draw a map showing how to get from one of the states you chose on Day 1 of this week to the other state you chose. If there isn't enough room on this page, feel free to use a larger paper.

Year 1 - Week 32 - Day 1

Review your research up to this point. Choose one southern state and one western state that you've researched to write about this week. Write the names of the states on the line below.

_____

You will be writing about these states for the rest of the week.

Year 1 - Week 32 - Day 2

On the following lines, write what you find most interesting about the states that you chose yesterday.

_____

_____

_____

_____

_____

_____

_____

_____

_____

_____

_____

_____

_____

_____

_____

Year 1 - Week 32 - Day 3

On the following lines, list similarities between the two states that you chose on Day 1 of this week.

_____

_____

_____

_____

_____

_____

_____

_____

_____

_____

_____

_____

_____

_____

_____

_____

Year 1 - Week 32 - Day 4

On the following lines, list differences between the two states that you chose on Day 1 of this week.

_____

_____

_____

_____

_____

_____

_____

_____

_____

_____

_____

_____

_____

_____

_____

_____

Year 1 - Week 32 - Day 5

Draw a map showing how to get from one of the states you chose on Day 1 of this week to the other state you chose. If there isn't enough room on this page, feel free to use a larger paper.

Year 1 - Week 33 - Day 1

Review your research up to this point. Choose one southern state and one eastern state that you've researched to write about this week. Write the names of the states on the line below.

_____

You will be writing about these states for the rest of the week.

Year 1 - Week 33 - Day 2

On the following lines, write what you find most interesting about the states that you chose yesterday.

_____

_____

_____

_____

_____

_____

_____

_____

_____

_____

_____

_____

_____

_____

_____

_____

Year 1 - Week 33 - Day 3

On the following lines, list similarities between the two states that you chose on Day 1 of this week.

_____

_____

_____

_____

_____

_____

_____

_____

_____

_____

_____

_____

_____

_____

_____

_____

Year 1 - Week 33 - Day 4

On the following lines, list differences between the two states that you chose on Day 1 of this week.

_____

_____

_____

_____

_____

_____

_____

_____

_____

_____

_____

_____

_____

_____

_____

_____

Year 1 - Week 33 - Day 5

Draw a map showing how to get from one of the states you chose on Day 1 of this week to the other state you chose. If there isn't enough room on this page, feel free to use a larger paper.

Year 1 - Week 34 - Day 1

Review your research up to this point. Choose one northern state and one eastern state that you've researched to write about this week. Write the names of the states on the line below.

_____

You will be writing about these states for the rest of the week.

Year 1 - Week 34 - Day 2

On the following lines, write what you find most interesting about the states that you chose yesterday.

_____

_____

_____

_____

_____

_____

_____

_____

_____

_____

_____

_____

_____

_____

Year 1 - Week 34 - Day 3

On the following lines, list similarities between the two states that you chose on Day 1 of this week.

_____

_____

_____

_____

_____

_____

_____

_____

_____

_____

_____

_____

_____

_____

_____

Year 1 - Week 34 - Day 4

On the following lines, list differences between the two states that you chose on Day 1 of this week.

_____

_____

_____

_____

_____

_____

_____

_____

_____

_____

_____

_____

_____

_____

_____

Year 1 - Week 34 - Day 5

Draw a map showing how to get from one of the states you chose on Day 1 of this week to the other state you chose. If there isn't enough room on this page, feel free to use a larger paper.

Year 1 - Week 35 - Day 1

Review your research up to this point. Choose one northern state and one western state that you've researched to write about this week. Write the names of the states on the line below.

_____

You will be writing about these states for the rest of the week.

Year 1 - Week 35 - Day 2

On the following lines, write what you find most interesting about the states that you chose yesterday.

_____

_____

_____

_____

_____

_____

_____

_____

_____

_____

_____

_____

_____

_____

_____

_____

_____

_____

Year 1 - Week 35 - Day 3

On the following lines, list similarities between the two states that you chose on Day 1 of this week.

_____

_____

_____

_____

_____

_____

_____

_____

_____

_____

_____

_____

_____

_____

_____

Year 1 - Week 35 - Day 4

On the following lines, list differences between the two states that you chose on Day 1 of this week.

_____

_____

_____

_____

_____

_____

_____

_____

_____

_____

_____

_____

_____

_____

_____

_____

_____

Year 1 - Week 35 - Day 5

Draw a map showing how to get from one of the states you chose on Day 1 of this week to the other state you chose. If there isn't enough room on this page, feel free to use a larger paper.

Year 1 - Week 36 - Day 1

Review your research up to this point. Look over all of the states that you've researched. You will be writing about these states for the rest of the week.

Year 1 - Week 36 - Day 2

On the following lines, write what you find most interesting, collectively, about the states that you've researched.

_____

_____

_____

_____

_____

_____

_____

_____

_____

_____

_____

_____

_____

_____

_____

Year 1 - Week 36 - Day 3

On the following lines, list similarities between the states that you've researched.

_____

_____

_____

_____

_____

_____

_____

_____

_____

_____

_____

_____

_____

_____

_____

_____

_____

_____

Year 1 - Week 36 - Day 4

On the following lines, list differences between the states that you've researched.

_____

_____

_____

_____

_____

_____

_____

_____

_____

_____

_____

_____

_____

_____

_____

_____

Year 1 - Week 36 - Day 5

On the following lines, write which state you've enjoyed learning about the most and why.

_____

_____

_____

_____

_____

_____

_____

_____

_____

_____

_____

_____

_____

_____

_____

_____

Congratulations on finishing Year 1!

Keep up the good work in Year 2!

To purchase additional copies of this book, *Self-Learning U.S. History & Geography with Creative Writing and Art: Workbook 2*, or other books by Randi, search for Randi Millward on Amazon, or request books by Randi at your local bookstore.

For whosoever shall call upon the name of the Lord shall be saved.

Romans 10:13